Welcome to the innocent childhood of my aunt, Norma Dell. Norma's father homesteaded on a mountain ranch in Northwest Colorado in the mid-1900s, and that is where Norma grew up. It was a world without electricity or indoor plumbing. They cooked and heated with a wood stove. They lived happily in a simple world. They worked hard and enjoyed clean living. Elk, deer, and many mountain creatures surrounded them. Norma loved her outdoor life and especially her horse, Croppy.

She was honest, loving, and a great storyteller. There were many stories about her childhood. I hope you enjoy looking into a small window of her life.

To my Aunt Norma, who inspired this book, and to every child who dreams of having a horse.

Written by: Bethany Gardner-Rose
Illustrations by: Peggy Badour
Epilogue: Tracy Lawson
Contributor: Jim Gardner
Edited by: Clint Gardner and Lynn Sims

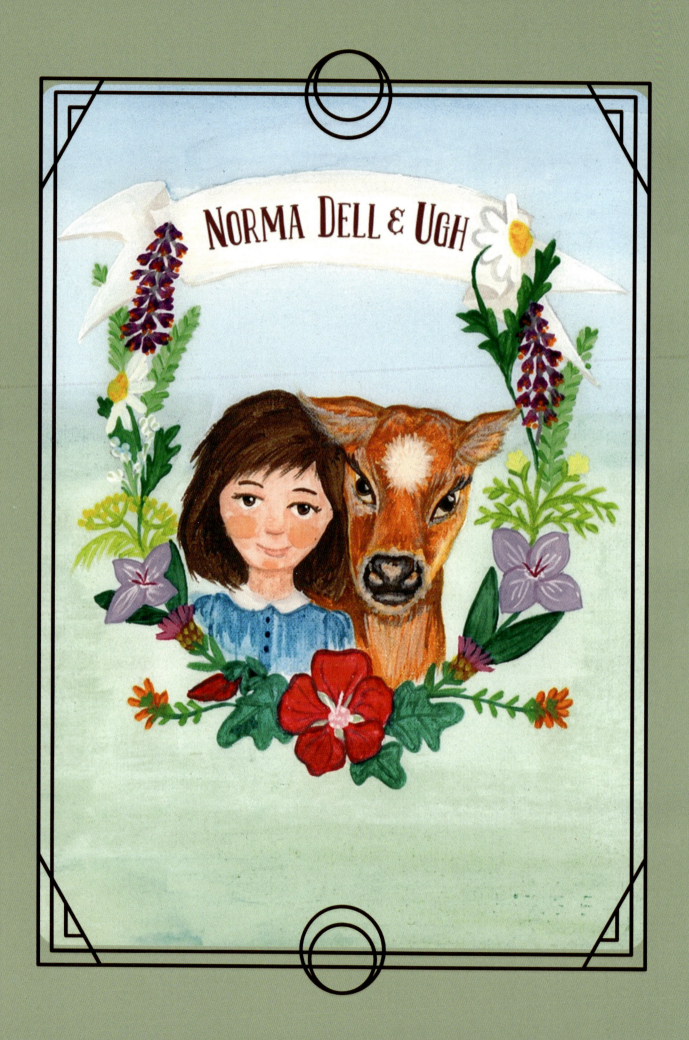

Good morning, Daddy," Norma chirped.

"Good morning!" replied Daddy as he bent down to kiss Norma's cheek.

"Daddy, will we bring cattle down from the mountain today?" Norma asked.

"No, honey, first thing in the morning," Daddy said.

"Oh boy! Will Shorty be there?"

"He sure will. He's my right-hand man. Norma, you get ol' Sam ready to ride tomorrow."

Norma had been riding her black quarter horse, Sam, since she was four years old. He was never in a hurry and was easy to catch in the pasture.

"Did you get the eggs yet?" Daddy took his coat from the door, saying, "It's time to start our day, honey." "No, sir," Norma answered. "Well, go on then and wear a jacket." Norma grabbed her jacket and darted out the door.

"Hello!" said Norma as she stopped at the edge of the step to pet Thom Thumb, a mostly white Australian Shepherd with a brown face and white nose. "Now, that's a good boy."

Norma was quickly back on task to gather eggs with Thom Thumb following. She took a bucket of chicken scratch from the shelf, reached her tiny hand into the bucket, and scattered the scratch on the ground.

"Here, chick, here, chick," Norma called. The chickens ran from the coop and started pecking at their morning treat. Norma and Thom Thumb went into the coop to gather the eggs. "Only four eggs this morning, Thom. Daddy won't be happy," Norma said.

The afternoon had warmed nicely, and there was no longer a need for Norma to wear her jacket. She made her way to the barn and filled her pockets with horse treats. She yanked at Sam's halter, which was on a hook too high for her to reach, and it dropped to the ground.

Picking it up, she said, "Sam, Sam, come on now," as she kept the halter tucked behind her back, as Daddy had taught her. Sam trotted over at the sight of her held-out hand full of treats. While Sam nibbled at the treats.

Norma took the halter and slipped it over Sam's head. Knowing that he had been caught, Sam sighed deeply, and Norma smiled.

———————— ♥ ————————

Norma rode Sam all afternoon, first past the frog pond and then down the trail toward Daddy's cabins. Daddy had built two cabins when he first moved to the mountain. She liked seeing them and imagining what it might have been like when he lived in them.

Norma saw a large rock and decided to use it to get off Sam. She guided him toward the rock and slipped down, still holding the lead rope. She jumped off the rock with a thud. Norma looked up at Sam, tugged at his halter, and brought his muzzle close to her face. "I love you, Sam!"

Norma and Sam walked along together for a bit. Sam paused now and then to munch on the sprouting grass. It was always exciting to look for arrowheads when at the cabins. Norma searched, turning over rocks and peeking under bushes and cactus plants.

With the lead rope in hand, she began tugging at Sam to follow her. Norma looked around for the nearest fence, and Sam obediently followed her. She climbed to the top rail and then swung herself onto Sam's back. She held the lead rope tight and gently guided Sam toward the red dirt road. As the tall horse trotted along, Norma ran her fingers through his mane. With a slight kick and squeeze of her legs, they headed for home.

When Norma got home, she took Sam back to the pasture. Then, she worked alongside Daddy while he did the evening chores. Their work was just completed when Mommy hollered, "Supper's ready!" They were all Norma's favorites: buckskin steak, homegrown green beans, and biscuits.

The next morning, the barnyard rooster crowed loud and clear. Norma stretched her legs, rubbed her eyes, and yawned big. She sat straight up in bed as she felt someone tickling her feet. "Hi Daddy!" Norma squealed, now sitting crisscross applesauce.

Daddy grinned, saying, "Time to get up! We need to get the cattle down the mountain today. Shorty will be here soon, and we'll be heading out."

Norma bounded from her bed. "Yes, I'll be ready!"

Norma put on her blue jeans, turned up at the ankles, her western shirt with red checks, and brown cowboy boots. Her hat was tan with red trim around the brim. Shorty was at the table drinking coffee with Daddy and Mommy when Norma came into the kitchen. Scrambled eggs, toast, and a glass of juice were sitting on the table for Norma. She ate every bite of breakfast, knowing there would be no stopping for lunch and supper would be hours away. Daddy put his coffee cup in the sink and headed out the door. Norma looked at Shorty for the go-sign, and he gave her a wink.

Once mounted on their horses, Daddy and Shorty rode ahead of Norma. Sam had no interest in rushing. Norma did her best but Sam would have none of it.

Norma hollered, "Wait for me!"

After several hours of riding, they found the herd, and Shorty made camp.

He gathered firewood and began making cornmeal mush for supper. This would also serve as breakfast and lunch for the rest of the journey.

———— ♥ ————

"Can I help?" asked Norma. "Yes, kid, you sure can," replied Shorty as he added water to a pan over the fire.

Norma took the bag of cornmeal from Shorty's saddlebag and carefully poured the cornmeal into a tin cup. Shorty took the cup and tipped the contents into the hot water and stirred it until it was thick. The first night, Shorty opened a can of milk and poured it over the mush. Norma never acquired a taste for canned milk, so Shorty sprinkled a little sugar on hers. After dinner, with a full tummy, Norma crawled into her sleeping bag. Within minutes, she was sound asleep.

When Norma opened her eyes the next morning, she saw Daddy pouring cowboy coffee. Shorty was cutting the cornmeal mush into slices for them. Norma stretched and crawled out of her sleeping bag. She pulled on her boots, combed through her hair, and sat on an old log next to Daddy.

"Good morning. How's my little girl?" Daddy asked proudly.

"Good and hungry!" Norma replied. Shorty chuckled, putting a piece of cornmeal on a tin plate.

───────── ♥ ─────────

"I have a surprise for you this morning," Shorty said. He drizzled maple syrup on Norma's cornmeal and handed her the plate. It was sweet, warm, and delicious.

The day turned into a long one for Norma. The cattle seemed to have scattered all over the face of the mountain. Mama cows and their calves hid in the bushes. The bulls sensed a change coming, so they did their best to stay hidden. Norma trotted Sam to a small knoll and looked out, hoping to catch a glimpse of Daddy. She searched in every direction but couldn't see him anywhere. Norma felt anxious and steered Sam along the course of the river. Sam must have been thirsty because he seemed to trot a little faster at the sight of a good drink.

When they got to the river, feeling uneasy, she slid off Sam and told him they would need to find Daddy. Sam continued drinking, not seeming a bit worried. Norma climbed her way back onto Sam, patted him, and turned him sharply back toward the herd.

As she got closer to the herd, she could see the sparkle of Daddy's silver spurs in the sunshine. Much to her relief, Daddy was there waiting for her: "Honey, come with me."

Norma held firmly to the reins, and with a tug to the left, she cued Sam to follow Daddy. The ground grew thick with weeds and brush the farther they went from the soft, grassy area. Daddy got off his horse, Gizmo, the once-wild mustang. He reached up to help Norma down.

"Honey, we have an orphaned calf. We need to find him and give him a bottle," he said soberly.

As they walked with their horses, Daddy looked toward the ground, looking for the small calf. Norma stayed close behind him, placing each of her steps in her Daddy's boot-prints.

———————— ♥ ————————

They were fighting their way through the thickets when Daddy stopped. He bent down on one knee and grinned, "Here he is." He made a sweep with his arm through the tall weeds, and there, tucked in deep, was a baby calf. "He was born this morning; Norma, his mama, didn't make it."

Daddy scooped him up and laid him on the front of his saddle. He picked up Norma, put her back on Sam, and they headed back to camp.

"I'll take care of him, Daddy, I promise I will!" Norma pleaded, sitting next to the calf and stroking his coat. He was brown and white, his ears warm and fuzzy. Norma loved his big brown eyes and long eyelashes.

"I'll take care of you," said Norma and kissed his head. The little calf looked up at his newly adopted mother and let out an "ugh." Norma and Daddy laughed at the little calf's inability to moo.

So, with that, Norma named her calf "Ugh" and so began the friendship of Norma Dell and Ugh.

———————— ♥ ————————

Clip-clop, clip-clop. Norma found herself looking at the back of her Daddy's shirt. Norma's horse, Sam, took his time. She gave Sam a gentle squeeze with her legs, leaned forward and clicked her tongue, "click, click, click. But Sam kept his slow and steady pace. Daddy's horse, Gizmo, trotted ahead, much faster.

Once back at the homestead, Daddy dismounted Gizmo and led him to the barn, and Norma rode Sam to the fence. "Come on, Sam," she said in a frustrated tone. Norma lifted her leg over the saddle. She put her boot on the fence and stepped back onto the red dirt. "For heaven's sake, Sam, you're the slowest horse that ever was!" Norma complained, as she loosened the cinch strap. Taking off Sam's saddle, she led him to the pasture. Sam happily obliged, taking no notice that his pace was upsetting to his young rider. Her small hand took off Sam's halter, and she slipped the buckle loose. Reaching up, she gave Sam's rump a pat, urging, "Go on then!"

Turning from the pasture, Norma headed out to play with Ugh, her pet calf. She whistled toward the grazing cattle and clapped her hands. Ugh looked up from the blowing, rippling grass and quickly came running to her. His brown and white spotted coat looked soft and shiny in the sun. Norma and Ugh played for hours that afternoon. When the sun grew too warm, Norma retreated to her playhouse.

Daddy had made the perfect playhouse for her. Inside, the walls were white. A border of horses ran around the ceiling, circling the entire room. Posters of her favorite cowboys and cowgirls were hung with pride around the playhouse. She had a small wooden chair with a padded seat and ruffles around the edges. A small bed was along one wall, covered by a beautiful blanket with pink horses. Norma was on her bed, fluffing her pillow and reading Annie's Cowboy Tales. Then, she heard voices outside.

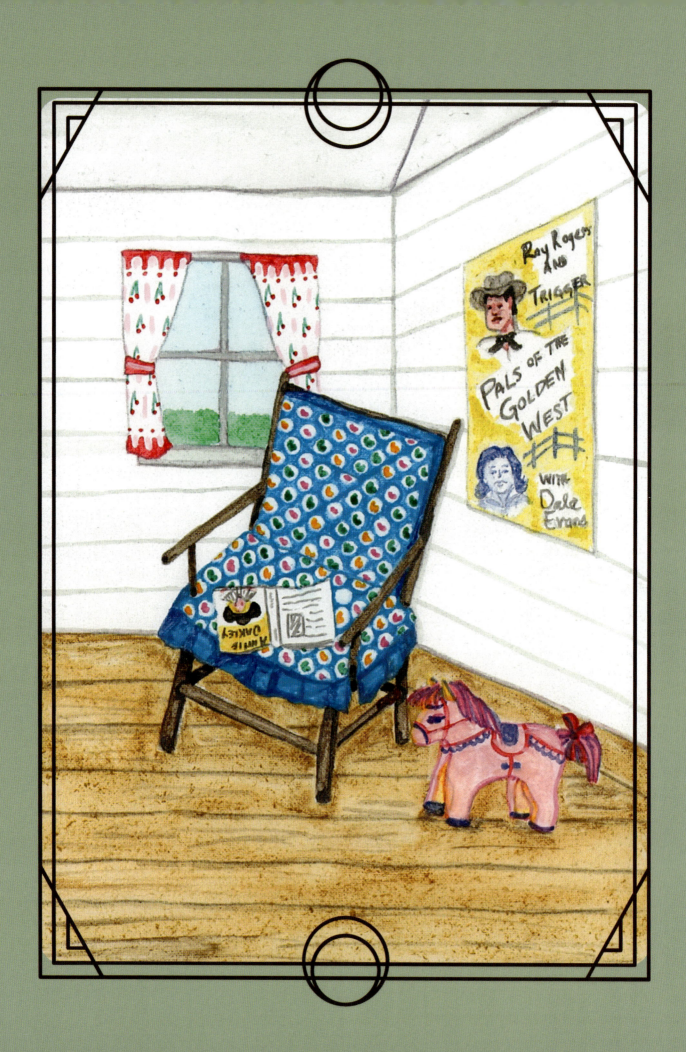

It was rare that they had visitors at their cabin, so she wondered who it could be. She hopped off the bed and peeked out of the small window.

It was Miss Gracie leading Croppy. Miss Gracie had her own ranch nearby and loved the independence and adventure of living in the West.

Norma dashed out the door and ran to stand by Daddy. Miss Gracie smiled broadly at Norma as she held out the reins. "Croppy is for you, Norma."

Miss Gracie had watched Norma work with her Daddy on horseback. She knew Norma worked hard, and Miss Gracie admired it. This generous gift overwhelmed Norma. Croppy was a tall horse with a chestnut coat, and he had a white star on his forehead. One back hoof was white, and he had kind, cocoa-brown eyes. Croppy served as the tutor horse for mountain children. Norma had previously ridden him at Miss Gracie's ranch. Croppy knew how to drive cattle, and he could easily match Daddy's pace. "Thank you, Miss Gracie, thank you very much!" cheered Norma as she patted Croppy's shoulder and leaned against him.

Daddy smiled, pleased with the response from this well-mannered horse. Daddy had a high-back saddle that Norma could ride on. He always made sure the stirrups were down as far as they could go. Norma used the stirrups to help her mount Sam or Croppy, but not while she rode. Daddy would not let her ride with stirrups until he knew she could ride a horse well. It took a great deal of effort for young Norma to mount a horse by herself. She would use the stirrups but generally would have to find a fence or rock to climb up on.

———————— ♥ ————————

One afternoon, a local rancher, Mr. George, was visiting Daddy. He watched Norma as she led Croppy to the wooden fence and climbed aboard him. Mr. George went over to his horse and removed the saddle strings from his saddle. Riders use saddle strings to attach gear to the saddle. He then tied the strings to Norma's saddle horn, and they hung down far enough for Norma to reach them. The back of her saddle had long black saddle strings, but she had never used them to mount a horse before. Mr. George gave her a lesson on the new way to mount Croppy. It would allow her to get on him no matter where she was.

"Okay, darlin', first you grab the front strings in your left hand, then the back strings in your right hand. There you go! Now, swing a bit and start climbing!"

With his hands on his hips, grinning from ear to ear, Mr. George stood back and watched Norma. She tightly grabbed the strings and swung her small frame back and forth. For a moment, she was under Croppy. Then, with a second swing, she got her foot in the stirrup. That boost helped her scramble up on her horse. Daddy had watched Norma proudly as she sat tall on Croppy. She looked down at Mr. George and said, "This is great!" Norma stretched out her arm, drawing her fingers through Croppy's mane.

Norma tugged the reins toward the open pasture, and with a little kick of her boot, she and Croppy were gone. From the first minute she got in the saddle with Croppy, she felt the trust that only a rider of a fine horse can feel. Norma fell in love with him almost immediately.

They spent hours together. Norma would climb all over him, and on a warm day they would play in the woodlands. He was the best horse a little girl could ever have, and they became the best of friends.

──────────── ♥ ────────────

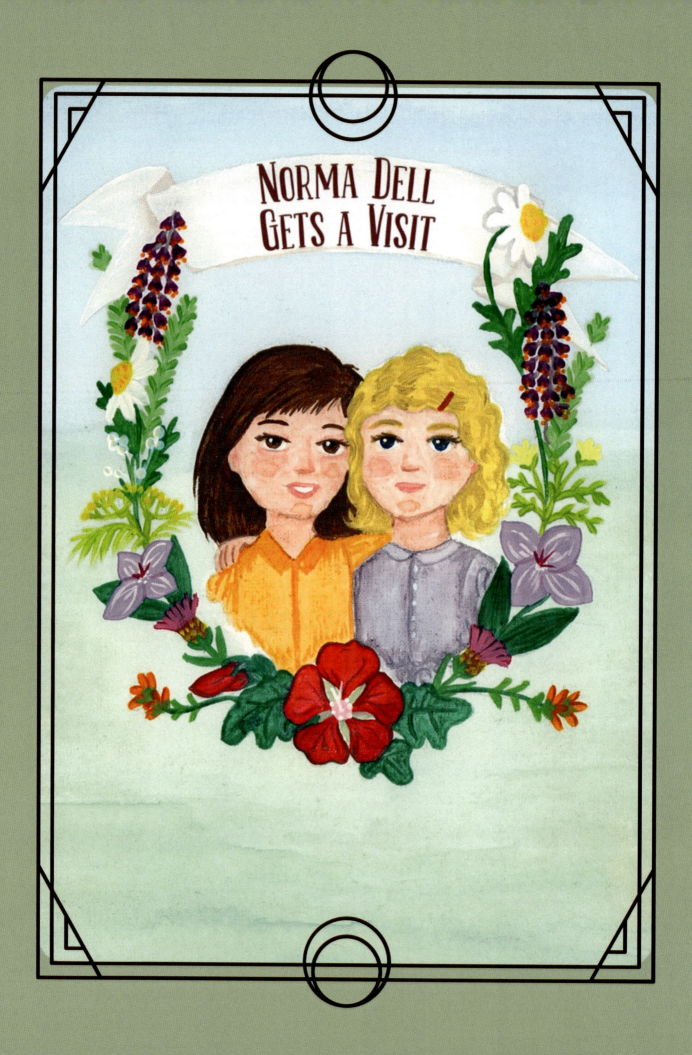

Norma's little fingers cupped Croppy's face and brought it close to hers. "Daddy hurt my feelings!" she sobbed as she told Croppy her sad story. "I didn't mean to make him mad."

Norma let go of Croppy's halter, but he stayed close. Her horse listened to every word she said, and she felt he was always on her side. She kissed the chocolate-brown nose of her loyal horse and pressed her face against his. The air was cold, but Croppy's coat felt warm. Norma climbed aboard her sweet boy, putting her hands under his mane. With tears running down her cheeks, she told him, "I love you, Croppy." Knowing that Daddy was upset with her, Norma shortened her afternoon ride.

"Norma, I'm not going to tell you again. Your chores come first!" Daddy had said firmly that morning, but she was anxious to go riding.

Her daily chores were straightforward. She washed the breakfast dishes, then fed the chickens. After that, she gathered the eggs. Today she had chosen to overlook her chores, and now she felt remorseful. Norma never wanted to disappoint Daddy or Mommy. Norma gave Croppy's belly a light kick, snapped the reins, and his trot turned into a full gallop. Her cowboy hat blew in the wind, staying on only because of the hat straps. She loved to gallop Croppy, feeling like they were one and part of the wind itself.

"Whoa!" shouted Norma as they curved around the pasture. "Whoa, boy!" She reined him back to a trot and headed for home.

Norma could see that Daddy was busy at the corral with his horse, Gizmo. She led Croppy to the trailhead. He followed the trail he knew so well and confidently brought them home.

———————— ♥ ————————

"Hi Daddy, are you still mad at me?" Her father walked over to her and gently replied, "No, honey, I'm not mad at you. Remember, chores first, riding and playing second," he reminded her.

Daddy was a quiet man; he wasn't tall, but he was stout and strong. He took excellent care of her and Mommy. Norma loved him and the life he provided for them.

"We have company coming tomorrow," Daddy said. Norma leaned forward on Croppy, holding tightly to the reins. Norma swung her right leg over Croppy's back. She bent her knees a bit, then let her feet touch the ground.

"I'm excited to see Jimmy and Carole!" she exclaimed while taking off Croppy's saddle. Norma's brother's children were about her age, making them not only her niece and nephew, but also her playmates. When Norma had company, she always went to bed early.

Tomorrow can't come soon enough," she said, kissing her Daddy goodnight. "Goodnight, honey. You get a good night's sleep," he whispered while tucking the blankets in around her. When the first ray of sun peeked in her window, Norma was awake.

She promptly ate her breakfast and completed her chores. "My goodness, little one, you made quick work of your chores this morning," Daddy said, smiling.

"Oh, yes, sir, I plan to sit right here on the fence and wait for Jimmy and Carole to get here." The old pickup drove in sooner than expected. Dust from the wheel wells hadn't settled when out popped two smiling faces! Norma hugged them both tightly.

Without hesitation, the compadres were off and running to the cabin to make a picnic lunch. Norma opened a loaf of her Mom's homemade bread. She spread peanut butter and jelly on every slice. Carole went to work filling up three mason jars with lemonade. The team tasked Jimmy with putting lids on each jar, good and tight. Cheerfully, Norma placed the three lunches in a saddlebag, and they raced out the door to saddle the horses.

Norma was on Croppy. Carole rode Goldie, a stunning palomino. Jimmy chose Jake, a dashing white quarter horse. Norma led the three of them to the path behind the cabin.

   This route would take them up a hill covered with red boulders, cedar trees, and sagebrush. The blue sky was a beautiful backdrop to a land that held endless possibilities.

   She told them the Native Americans once walked there, seeing the same silver-green sagebrush. Curious, Carole picked a few leaves from the bush. She rubbed them between her palms and took a deep breath. Norma looked at Carole's round face, her rosy cheeks and the soft blonde curls resting on her shoulders. 'Sagebrush can live over a hundred years when it grows wild,' Norma explained. She thought how sweet and quiet Carole was as they rode through the brush. Jimmy was tall and slender, had an ornery grin, and Norma knew he was a bit of a city boy. Deciding to take a break, they dismounted from their horses.

———— ♥ ————

"Now Jimmy, you go stand over in that clearing," Norma said in a firm tone as she pointed straight ahead. Jimmy happily followed instructions and sprinted to the clearing. With that, Norma took her lasso and got it spinning. Carole watched quietly, unsure of what was about to happen. Norma had a big grin on her face, the lasso going around and around, and with a flick of her hand, let it go. It twirled in the air and, with 100% accuracy, landed under Jimmy's feet. With a quick drawback of Norma's arm, the rope wrapped tight around his ankles.

Before he knew it, he was lying face flat on the ground. Norma let out a belly laugh and looked over at Carole. Her face was one of surprise, but hearing Norma's laughter, she couldn't help but laugh, too. Jimmy sat up, wrestled the rope off his ankles, stood up quickly, and dusted himself off. "Aw gee, it's not that funny!" But once the sting wore off, he chuckled too.

Norma decided it was time for lunch. She took the saddlebag from Croppy and shared the sandwiches. Happy to be together, they talked about horses and "cowboys and Indians." They gazed over the vast open terrain. "Let's take a ride to Cedar Mountain," Norma suggested. There was plenty of daylight left, and no one wanted the fun to end. The ride wasn't far, and the view from the top was stunning. They would take in every bit of beauty before heading back down the mountain. Norma was an excellent rider and always comfortable in the saddle. Jimmy leaned back in his seat on the way down. Carole looked uneasy and held tight to the reins, never taking her eyes off the path ahead.

As the three of them descended the mountain, they could hear bleating from a flock of sheep. As they got closer to the bottom, they saw men on horseback. They were tending the sheep, while dogs ran in and out among the animals, nipping at their hindquarters. The men were steering the sheep toward a distant canyon.

——————————— ♥ ———————————

Norma suddenly hopped off and knelt in the sagebrush, her hands gripping the reins. There lay a newborn lamb. Jimmy also dismounted and said, "I bet he got lost from that flock of sheep." As she mounted Croppy, Norma said, "Yes, I'm sure he did. Hand him up to me, Jimmy."

Jimmy gently picked up the little white lamb and Norma laid it across her lap. Carole felt badly for the orphaned lamb. Just a few soft bleats came from the stray. They guided their horses down to the sheep at the bottom of the mountain.

The sheepherders cheerily greeted the children and were very pleased to see the lamb. "Thank you for getting this little bugger back to us," one of the riders said. He tipped his hat and scratched his forehead. The children felt proud to have saved the fragile lamb. They waved goodbye to the sheepherders as Norma led the three of them toward home.

Carole lagged, taking a final look back, hoping to get one more glimpse of the baby lamb. There he was, with his mama, eagerly making up for missing his last meal. Carole smiled, her heart no longer heavy, knowing the lamb was cared for and goodbyes were not forever. The dusty cowboy gave a final wave to the little girl with rosy cheeks, blonde curls, and a big heart.

At the homestead, they all came together at the table. They feasted on a hearty meal of fried chicken, mashed potatoes, gravy, biscuits, hand-churned butter, and chokecherry jelly. They felt a deep sense of satisfaction after a long day exploring Norma's beautiful, vast backyard.

These are memories that the three children would carry in their hearts for the rest of their lives. Best friends, today, tomorrow, and forever.

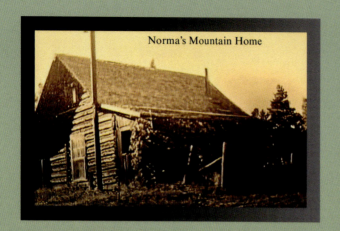

Epilogue Written By:
Tracy Lawson, daughter of Norma Dell.

Ugh the Calf

 I don't remember how old my mom was, but she told me a story once of a calf that didn't have a mama to take care of him, so she had to take care of the calf. She learned how to feed the calf with a bottle, and she decided to name him Ugh, because he didn't really make a calf sound; it was more like a grunting sound. Ugh was really cute as a calf and they played together all summer long. But then it was time for mom to go to school in Brown's Park, so she and her mom moved off of the mountain for the winter. After the snow melted from the mountain, they moved back to the mountain where Ugh was waiting for my mom. He came running when he saw her, but he was much larger than my mom remembered. He had grown very quickly over the winter.

Croppy the Horse

    Croppy was a really good kid horse that was given to my mom. He had been passed along from kid to kid around Brown's Park because he was such a gentle horse and, most of all, a friend to all the kids. He was a great horse for kids to learn how to ride. The funny thing about Croppy is that he was scared of men and most grownups. My mom and Croppy were truly best friends, and they had a lot of really good times together. When my mom was sad, she would always go out to the corrals and talk to Croppy and sometimes Ugh about what was making her sad. She found that Croppy and Ugh were both amazing friends and very good listeners.

———— ♥ ————

Jimmy and Carole

Jim and Carole were my mom's nephew and niece, but they were all so close in age, it was more like they were actually brother and sister to my mom. They were also very close to one another, and they spent a lot of time together riding horses and going on fishing trips with my mom's dad and Jim and Carole's dad. My mom had a very special place in her heart for Jim and Carole, even after they were all grown up and had families of their own, and they stayed in close contact with one another. I always remember the stories she told us as we were growing up about Jim and Carole and so many other people that she loved.

My mom has passed away and now lives with Jesus, and although we miss her each and every day, we also know that she's spending time with her dad, her brother, her beloved horse Croppy, and her calf Ugh.